MACEDONIAN CHIDLREN'S BOOK

COLORS AND SHAPES

FOR YOUR KIDS

AUTHOR
ROAN WHITE

ILLUSTRATIONS
FEDERICO BONIFACINI

Црвена

Сина

Жолта

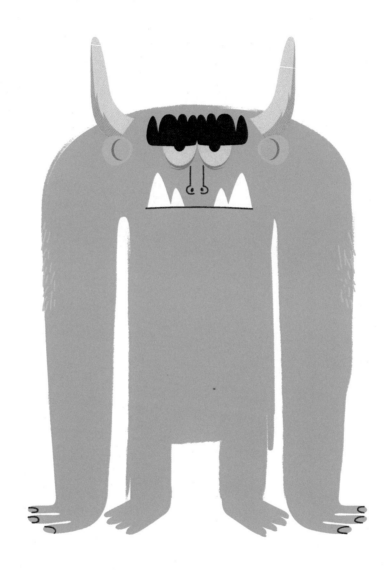

Зелена

Портокалова

Виолетова

Бела

Црна

Кафена

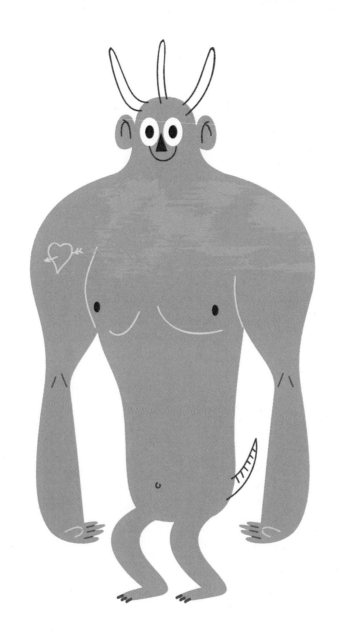

Розева

Сива

Триаголник

Круг

Квадрат

Правоаголник

Ромб

Паралелограм

Трапез

Дијамант

Пентагон

Хексагон

Октагон